The Ram Mindset: Building Discipline, Purpose and Resilience in Daily Life

Step-by-step principles from Ramayana for today's working professionals, entrepreneurs and changemakers

NIKHIL KUMAR

BlueRose ONE
Stories Matter
New Delhi • London

BLUEROSE PUBLISHERS
India | U.K.

For permissions requests or inquiries regarding this publication, please contact:

BLUEROSE PUBLISHERS
www.BlueRoseONE.com info@bluerosepublishers.com
+91 8882 898 898
+4407342408967

ISBN: 978-93-7542-618-9

First Edition: December 2025

DEDICATION

To the timeless wisdom of Lord Ram and to every reader seeking balance, purpose and strength in a changing world.

DISCLAIMER

This book, The Ram Mindset: Building Discipline, Purpose and Resilience in Daily Life, is an interpretive work inspired by the timeless lessons of the Ramayana. It is meant to share practical insights and values for modern life, not as a scholarly, theological, or definitive commentary on the life of Lord Ram or the Ramayana itself. The author has strived to treat the subject matter with utmost respect and sensitivity. Any unintended errors or omissions are deeply regretted. Readers are encouraged to approach this work as a perspective on applying age-old principles to today's world, rather than a religious guide. The author and publisher disclaim any liability for decisions or actions taken by readers based on the content of this book. All references to characters, places and stories from the Ramayana are made with profound reverence for the cultural and spiritual significance they hold.

CONTENTS

	Acknowledgment	1
1	Anchored in Dharma — Living by Your Core Values	3
2	Dharma in Decision-Making — Leading with Clarity in a Complex World	11
3	Emotional Mastery — Responding with Strength, Not Reacting with Stress	17
4	Discipline as Devotion — Cultivating Focus and Consistency Like Ram	23
5	Leading with Purpose — The Ramayana Blueprint for Modern Leadership	31
6	Purpose-Driven Action — How Ram's Clarity of Mission Inspires Modern Leadership	39
7	Resilience in Chaos — How Ram Overcame Exile, Loss and War with Grace	47
8	Purpose and Patience — Walking the Long Road with Grace	55
9	Modern-Day Vanvas: Handling Career Setbacks, Rejections & Transitions	61
10	Sita's Strength — Emotional Resilience, Dignity and Patience in Unfair Times	67
11	Ravan's Mind Psychology — What Ambition Without Dharma Leads To	73

12	The Power of Relationships — Building Trust, Loyalty and Support like Ram	79
13	Ram Rajya Within — Leading Teams with Fairness, Empathy and Strength	87
14	Lakshman's Loyalty — Commitment and Boundaries in Leadership	93
15	Bharata's Sacrifice: Selfless Leadership & Zero-Ego Management	101
16	Parents as Leaders: King Dashrath, Kaushalya & The Family Dharma System	107
17	The Mentor Mindset: Wisdom from Vashishtha & Vishwamitra	113
18	Lessons from Hanuman — The Power of Devotion, Humility and Relentless Action	119
19	Ram Rajya — Creating Harmony in Teams, Families and Communities	125
20	The Legacy of Ram — Living with Character, Even When No One Is Watching	133
21	Becoming Ram — Integrating Values, Leadership & Purpose in Modern Life	139
	About The Author	147

ACKNOWLEDGMENTS

This book has been a journey of deep reflection, discipline and learning. I offer my heartfelt gratitude to my family, mentors and friends—whose constant encouragement, faith and support gave me the strength to bring this vision to life.

My sincere respect to the timeless wisdom of the Ramayana, to the saints, scholars and storytellers who have preserved and passed forward the teachings of Lord Ram. Their guidance continues to illuminate countless lives, including mine. To every interaction, experience and moment that shaped my understanding---your influence is present in every page of this book.

And to you, the reader---thank you for choosing to walk this path of growth. May these insights help you connect with your own Ram Mindset and lead a life of purpose, resilience and righteousness.

Chapter 1

ANCHORED IN DHARMA — LIVING BY YOUR CORE VALUES

"Ragkukul reet sada chali aayi, praan jaaye par vachan na jaayi."

("The code of the Raghu clan is unchanging: one may lose his life, but never break his word.")

When Lord Ram agreed to leave Ayodhya for 14 years of exile on the very day he was to be crowned king, it wasn't a strategic decision. It was dharma in action—pure, powerful and non-negotiable.

This moment, etched in the soul of the Ramayana, isn't just a tale of sacrifice. It is a blueprint for integrity, a reminder that greatness begins with living by values, not convenience.

What Is Dharma?

In the simplest form, Dharma means the right way of living. It is duty, ethics, responsibility and self-discipline—guided by truth, not trend.

For Lord Ram, dharma wasn't abstract. It was clear, internalized and ever-present in his decisions as a son, a prince, a husband, a brother and a leader.

In the modern world, this translates to living by your principles, even when doing so is difficult. It means choosing long-term trust over short-term gain and character over comfort.

The Modern-Day Dilemma: Compromising Values for Quick Wins

Think about it:

- Have you ever said "yes" to something just to avoid conflict, even if it clashed with your values?
- Have you bent rules at work, skipped commitments, or rationalized dishonesty for the sake of results?
- Do you often feel the gap between who you are and who you're becoming?

Stress, burnout and dissatisfaction often don't come from hard work—they come from value conflicts.

When your external life doesn't reflect your internal compass, discontent grows. That's why anchoring your actions in dharma—as Ram did—is the first step toward peace and purpose.

Lesson from Ram: The Power of Value-Driven Choices

Ram's exile wasn't an act of weakness. It was the ultimate act of strength. In a single moment, he gave up power, comfort and ambition—for the sake of truth and loyalty.

As modern professionals, we don't face exile. But we face:

- Ethical dilemmas at work.
- Tough decisions between family and career.
- Pressure to perform, even if it means cutting corners

In these moments, the Ram Mindset reminds us:

✓ Never let convenience overrides your —1 Anchored in Dharma Living by Your Core Valuesconscience.

✓ The right thing is often not the easy thing—but it's always the lasting thing.

How to Apply This in Your Daily Life

Here's a step-by-step framework to build your own dharma compass:

1. **Define Your Core Values**

Take a moment to reflect:

- What are your non-negotiables? (e.g., honesty, reliability, compassion)
- What kind of person do you admire—and why?
- What actions make you feel proud of yourself?

Identify your 3–5 core values and keep them in clear view

2. Check for Alignment

Ask yourself daily:

- Did I act today in line with my values?
- Was there a moment I compromised—and why?
- What could I have done differently?

Awareness is the first step toward alignment.

3. Stand Firm in Difficult Moments

Before making a tough decision, pause and ask:

- Is this aligned with my core principles?
- Will I be at peace with this choice tomorrow?

This self-check builds moral clarity and emotional strength.

4. Create a Dharma Routine

Like Lord Ram, discipline isn't occasional—it's habitual.

- Set daily intentions rooted in your values.
- Let your calendar reflect your priorities—not just your tasks.

- Build systems (journaling, accountability partners, quiet time) to help stay centered.

Real-World Reflection: When Dharma Meets Business

Ritu, a startup founder, was offered a lucrative contract from a client who hinted at "creative reporting" to win investor trust. She declined—despite needing the money—because it violated her ethical framework. Six months later, the client was exposed. Her integrity saved her brand.

Aditya, a middle manager, was asked to cut employees under cost pressure. Instead of randomly selecting, he spent nights evaluating who truly depended on their job, advocating for alternatives. His team never forgot his fairness—and his reputation rose.

Both chose the Ram Mindset—dharma over drama, clarity over convenience.

Reflect & Practice

Journal Prompts:

1. What value do I want to be remembered for?
2. When was the last time I chose values over convenience?
3. Where am I currently out of alignment—and how can I course-correct?

Daily Practice:

- ✓ 3-minute "Dharma Check" before big meetings or decisions.
- ✓ Weekly reflection on choices that aligned or clashed with your values.

Closing Thought

Dharma doesn't make life easier—but it makes it honourable. It's what turned Ram from a prince into an ideal king.

And in the noise of today's world, it's what will turn you from a performer into a leader.

"Live not by the approval of others, but by the truth of your heart."

Begin here. Build within.

Chapter 2

DHARMA IN DECISION-MAKING — LEADING WITH CLARITY IN A COMPLEX WORLD

"When in doubt, follow your dharma — not your comfort."

In an age where choices are infinite and decisions are rushed, clarity has become a rare asset. Professionals, leaders and entrepreneurs are bombarded with daily dilemmas — from ethical trade-offs to personal sacrifices, to difficult people decisions.

Yet thousands of years ago, Lord Ram faced equally complex crossroads. He didn't just choose what was easy or beneficial — he chose what was right, rooted in his unwavering commitment to dharma (righteous duty).

This chapter will help you translate Ram's principle-based decision-making into your modern life — so you can lead with clarity, courage and conviction.

1. What Is Dharma, Really?

Dharma is often misinterpreted as religion or blind duty. But in the Ramayana, dharma is deeper — it's your true responsibility in any given role or context.

For Ram, being a son meant honoring his father's word. As a leader, it meant protecting his people. As a husband, it meant navigating duty with dignity.

Modern Insight: Dharma is role-based clarity — knowing what's right in context, not what's comfortable.

2. When Emotions Run High, Dharma Grounds You

Ram faced immense emotional conflict — leaving Ayodhya,

separating from Sita and fighting his own kin. Yet, he did not act out of rage, fear, or desire.

He paused. He reflected. He chose dharma over drama.

Modern Insight: In conflict, don't react emotionally. Respond with value-based reflection.

Try This: Before making a tough call, ask:

- What is my highest responsibility here?
- Who or what may be affected by this?
- What action aligns with integrity, even if it's hard?

3. Decision Fatigue vs. Value-Based Choices

In today's world, leaders suffer from decision fatigue. The Ram mindset simplifies this — anchor your decisions in principles, not pressure.

Ram didn't delay action because he feared judgment. He acted from a clear inner compass.

Modern Insight: Clarity isn't about having all the answers. It's about having unshakable values that filter your choices.

4. Ethics vs. Outcomes: Choosing the Inner Win

When Ram could have returned to Ayodhya immediately after Dasharatha's death, he still honored his father's word and completed the 14-year exile.

Why? Because he saw victory not in what he gained, but in who he remained.

Modern Insight: The real win is not success—it's integrity. Build a life where your values survive your victories.

Ask Yourself: " Will this decision make me proud 5 years from now ? "

Ram's Dharma Decision-Making Framework

Situation	**Ram's Decision**	**Dharma Lens Applied**
Father's promise vs. personal gain	Went into exile peacefully	Duty as a son over desire as a prince
Sita's exile due to public doubt	Made a painful personal choice	Dharma as a king vs. role as a husband
Ravana's brother defects	Listened and accepted Vibhishan	Justice and open-mindedness over prejudice

5. Practicing "Dharma Thinking" at Work

Scenario 1: Should I promote a high performer with poor ethics?
Dharma says: Integrity over output. Culture over short-term wins.

Scenario 2: I have to let someone go. Should I soften the truth?
Dharma says: Be kind, but transparent. Respect the person's dignity.

Scenario 3: I'm tempted to cut corners to meet deadlines.
Dharma says: Shortcuts may save time, but cost you trust.

Modern Application: When values and deadlines collide, choose the one you'll still respect at the end of your career.

A Simple Dharma Decision Tool (3Qs)

Before any major decision, pause and reflect:

1. Is this aligned with my deepest values?
2. Am I acting out of clarity, or out of fear/ego?
3. What would my highest self-choose in this moment?

Write these down. Build them into your decision routine. Let them shape your leadership.

Final Thought

Ram didn't always make easy choices. He made the right ones.

In your journey as a professional, entrepreneur, parent, or partner, you'll be tested. Clarity will waver. Pressure will mount. But if you root yourself in dharma — in conscious, courageous, values-based choices —you won't just lead.

You'll lead in a way that outlives your title.

Chapter 3

EMOTIONAL MASTERY — RESPONDING WITH STRENGTH, NOT REACTING WITH STRESS

"Na hum krodhi, na hi bhayankar; Ram naam japta banat sughar."

("Neither angry nor terrifying—chanting Ram's name refines even the wildest nature.")

In the world of Ramayana, Lord Ram remains the embodiment of grace under pressure. In situations that would overwhelm even the strongest minds—exile, betrayal, war and separation from loved ones—he stood steady, not because he lacked emotion, but because he had mastery over it.

In today's world of constant pressure, speed and uncertainty, emotional mastery is not a luxury—it's survival. Ram's example teaches us that real strength lies not in suppressing emotions but in choosing your response with awareness and discipline.

The Modern-Day Reality: Emotional Burnout Is Real

- A sudden email triggers anxiety.
- A team member's mistake causes frustration.
- Social media spirals comparison and insecurity.
- A personal setback leaves you emotionally drained, yet the workday must go on.

These situations are now common. But reacting with anger, blame, or panic often damages more than it fixes. That's where the Ram Mindset offers a path—responding with clarity and calm, not chaos.

Lessons from Ram: Emotional Strength Is Inner Governance

Let's look at how Lord Ram handled some of the most emotionally intense moments:

1. When exiled on the day of coronation
   Ram's response: Calm acceptance and immediate preparation.

Lesson: Do not resist what you cannot change. Instead, act with dignity and detachment.

2. When Sita was abducted
   Ram's response: Grief, followed by calm resolution to act.
   Lesson: Allow yourself to feel, but don't be consumed. Grief must fuel courage.

3. When he had to send Sita to the forest
   Ram's response: A painful decision made for the kingdom's dharma.
   Lesson: Emotional mastery sometimes means choosing duty over desire.

Each of these moments is emotionally charged. But Ram never let his reactions override his purpose. That is true leadership.

Emotional Triggers at Work (and What Would Ram Do?)

Situation	**Default Reaction**	**The Ram Mindset**
Criticism from a boss	Defensiveness or resentment	Reflect, absorb what's valid, stay calm
Colleague takes credit	Outburst or silent grudge	Address with grace and facts
Deadlines & burnout	Anxiety or blame	Prioritize, delegate, breathe, reset
Failure of a project	Guilt or shame	Learn, adapt and lead again

How to Build Emotional Mastery (The Ram Way)

1. Pause Before You React

Ram never made hasty decisions. Practice a short pause before responding:

- Take a deep breath.
- Ask: "Is this the best version of me responding?"
- Choose words from wisdom, not wounded ego.

2. Daily Practice of Self-Awareness

Like Ram meditated in the forest, you need space for silence:

- Start your day with 5 minutes of silence or mantra (Ram naam or breathwork).
- Journal your triggers and what you learned from them.
- This builds your emotional muscle.

3. Transform Emotion into Energy

Anger isn't bad—it's just raw energy. The Ram mindset channels it:

- Use anger to take constructive action.
- Use sadness to deepen empathy.
- Use fear to drive preparation.

4. Be the Stable One in the Room

Ram's calm made others trust him. Become that for your team:

- Speak less, listen more.
- Validate others' emotions without being swept by them.
- Practice "emotional mirroring" – respond at a slightly calmer level than what's coming at you.

Real-World Reflection: Emotionally Strong Leaders Are Trusted Leaders

Neha, a product head, faced an investor backlash after a failed feature launch. Instead of blaming her team, she accepted responsibility, calmly presented the learnings and realigned goals. Her team became more loyal—and investors respected her poise.

Ramesh, a father of two and a sales leader, meditates for 10 minutes daily before work. He noticed his decision-making became sharper and he could hold difficult conversations without stress.

Reflect & Practice

Journal Prompts:

1. What situations trigger my strongest emotional reactions?
2. How did I react last time—and what would Ram have done?
3. What practice can I adopt to increase my emotional space?

Daily Practice:

- ✓ Use the "Pause → Breathe → Respond" model once a day.
- ✓ Practice 3 minutes of silence or mantra before major tasks.
- ✓ End your day by reviewing one emotional victory—however small.

Closing Thought

Emotional mastery is not about being robotic. It's about knowing your emotional temperature and adjusting it by choice, not compulsion.

Lord Ram never avoided emotion—he transcended it. He turned grief into grace, anger into clarity and love into leadership.

"The one who governs himself first is fit to govern the world."
Learn to govern yourself. The world will follow.

Chapter 4

DISCIPLINE AS DEVOTION — CULTIVATING FOCUS AND CONSISTENCY LIKE RAM

"True discipline is not forced. It flows from devotion to one's purpose."

— Inspired by the life of Lord Ram

In an era of distractions, instant gratification and burnout, discipline has become the rarest superpower. While modern productivity books emphasize hacks and habits, Ram's life reveals something deeper—discipline born from devotion, not obligation.

Lord Ram's unwavering commitment to dharma (righteousness), even in hardship, reveals a mindset where routine is sacred, sacrifice is strength and focus is freedom.

What Is Discipline in the Ram Mindset?

To Ram, discipline wasn't about external control. It was internal alignment. Every choice—from obeying exile to preparing for war—was rooted in clarity of purpose and unshakable inner resolve.

- Discipline is not rigidity—it's rooted in self-respect.
- Discipline is not about suppression—it's about intentional living.
- Discipline is not punishment—it's freedom from chaos.

Let's explore how Ram's daily conduct, decisions and mindset offer a framework for sustained focus and calm progress, even in high-pressure environments.

1. Daily Rituals as Anchors of Stability

In exile, Lord Ram maintained a regulated routine despite uncertainty. He woke early, meditated, practiced archery and spent time with Sita and Lakshman. These simple rituals created inner order amid external chaos.

Modern Insight: When your external world is unstable (deadlines, pressure, setbacks), build consistency through small daily rituals—morning journaling, mindful meals, evening reflection. This grounds the mind.

2. Sacrifice: The Hidden Face of Discipline

Ram willingly gave up the luxuries of Ayodhya for 14 years in the forest—not out of compulsion, but out of love and moral clarity. He chose austerity to preserve family honor.

Modern Insight: True discipline often demands saying “No” to comfort. Sacrificing short-term ease for long-term growth is the essence of high-performing individuals—be it waking early, resisting impulse, or choosing values over convenience.

3. Focus on the Process, Not the Prize

Even during the toughest battles, Ram stayed present. His success wasn't in chasing results but in showing up with full awareness.

Modern Insight: We burn out chasing goals. Ram teaches us to honor the daily process—be it learning, building, or healing. Discipline becomes joyful when we detach from outcomes.

4. Self-Mastery Over External Control

When Lakshman was angry at Kaikeyi or Surpanakha, Ram stayed calm. He never reacted impulsively—he responded with thoughtful restraint.

Modern Insight: Today's professionals are judged not just by what they do, but how they respond under pressure. Discipline is the art of managing your inner world before influencing the outer one.

5. Consistency Over Intensity

Ram did not become "Ram" overnight. His strength came from years of training, service and patience. There were no shortcuts—just relentless consistency.

Modern Insight: In business, fitness, or personal growth, don't chase intense bursts. Choose sustainable consistency. Tiny steps daily beat rare heroic efforts.

The Ram Discipline Model

Here's a modern framework derived from Ram's approach:

Pillar	Practice	Daily Action Example
Clarity	Know why you're doing it	Write your purpose at the top of your to-do list
Rituals	Anchor your day	Begin the day with a 10-minute focus ritual
Restraint	Pause before reacting	Use a 5-second rule before replying/reacting
Reflection	Learn from each day	End the day with a quick self-check
Patience	Trust long-term growth	Measure effort, not just outcomes

A Story of Modern Discipline: From Chaos to Calm

Anirudh, a mid-level manager at a fast-paced fintech firm, often felt overwhelmed—emails, team issues, high expectations. After discovering Ram's story, he applied one change:

"Instead of doing more, I began my day like Ram—intentionally. I stopped checking email first. I started with a 15-minute clarity session—no distractions. Everything shifted."

He soon built morning and night rituals, blocked focused hours and reflected every Friday. His productivity soared and his stress fell drastically. He wasn't working harder—he was working like Ram: with intention.

Reflect & Practice

Ask Yourself:

- What is one area where I lack consistency?
- What distractions am I choosing over discipline?
- What would Ram do when tired, distracted, or discouraged?

Try This Weekly Practice:

1. Start Small: Choose one ritual (morning walk, no phone for first hour, journaling) and commit for 7 days.
2. Create a Sacred Hour: Block 1 distraction-free hour daily—label it "Ram Hour." Use it for your most meaningful task.
3. End with Reflection: Ask nightly: "Was I intentional today or reactive?" Note one win, one improvement.

Final Thought

Discipline isn't about iron will. It's about deep devotion to who you want to become. Lord Ram didn't become a revered figure because of one big moment—he earned that reverence by showing up daily with discipline and grace.

"Success isn't built in a moment. It's shaped by the moments you choose to stay disciplined—even when no one is watching."

Walk the disciplined path—not just to achieve more, but to live with more meaning, peace and power.

Chapter 5

LEADING WITH PURPOSE — THE RAMAYANA BLUEPRINT FOR MODERN LEADERSHIP

"A true leader walks last, listens first and acts only when it serves others."

– Inspired by the life of Lord Ram

In a world flooded with motivational quotes and leadership models, few offer a time-tested, values-driven blueprint quite like the life of Lord Ram. His leadership was not about domination or titles—it was about service, vision and dharma (righteous duty).

Whether you're a team lead, startup founder, policymaker, or student leader, purpose-driven leadership is what sets great leaders apart. Ram's journey through exile, war and kingship offers profound insights into leading with courage, empathy and clarity—even in the harshest conditions.

What Makes Ram a Timeless Leader?

Let's examine some defining traits of Lord Ram's leadership that are applicable even today:

1. Clarity of Purpose

From the forests to the battlefield, Ram never lost sight of his dharma. Every decision stemmed from a deep awareness of his higher purpose: to serve truth, protect the innocent and uphold balance.

Modern parallel: Great leaders don't chase short-term wins. They anchor decisions to core values and long-term vision.

2. Servant Leadership

Ram led from the front, never demanding obedience, but earning loyalty through humility and fairness. He took advice from everyone—rishi, soldier, even animals like Jatayu and Hanuman.

Modern parallel: In today's workplace, the best leaders listen deeply, empower others and create psychological safety.

3. Team First, Ego Last

During the war in Lanka, Ram made sure that every warrior had a role—from Hanuman to the smallest vanara (monkey). His army was united by purpose, not hierarchy.

Modern parallel: Great leaders celebrate collaboration over competition. They delegate wisely and uplift every contributor.

4. Decisive, Yet Compassionate

When faced with moral dilemmas—be it punishing Vali or handling Sita's return—Ram displayed a rare combination of firmness and empathy. He took time to reflect but acted when needed.

Modern parallel: Balanced leadership requires strong decision-making with emotional intelligence.

Leadership Lessons from Ram's Key Moments

Event	Leadership Action	Modern Application
Accepting 14 - year exile	Graceful transition of power, no resistance	Handle setbacks with poise and long-term focus

Event	Leadership Action	Modern Application
Building bridges (literally!)	Empowering Nala, Hanuman and team to solve problems	Delegate authority, trust your team's expertise
Dialogue with Vibhishan (Ravan's brother)	Valuing dissent, welcoming opposing views	Encourage open dialogue, embrace diversity of thought
Victory over Ravan	Focused on justice, not revenge	Stay mission-focused, avoid ego traps after success

The Ram Leadership Framework (for Modern Leaders)

Here's a practical 5-pillar model inspired by Lord Ram's leadership:

1. **Purpose (Dharma)**

Define your core mission beyond profits or promotions.
Ask: "What is the deeper value I serve through my work?"

2. **Presence**

Lead with attention. Be fully there—in meetings, conversations and crises.
Action: Practice mindful listening for 10 minutes a day.

3. People

Invest in people, not just outcomes.
Action: Recognize one teammate's effort daily. Build loyalty through respect.

4. Principles

Let values shape decisions—even tough ones.
Action: Create your non-negotiables (e.g., honesty, empathy, service).

5. Progress

Adapt, learn and lead with humility. Ram himself evolved across each stage.
Action: Ask for feedback. Reflect monthly on leadership wins and gaps.

Story Reflection: How "Ram-like" Leadership Transformed a Startup

Priya, the founder of a social enterprise, struggled with internal chaos—missed deadlines, miscommunication and rising attrition. After studying leadership through the Ramayana lens, she made subtle changes:

- Started weekly listening circles
- Publicly celebrated integrity, not just KPIs
- Delegated decisions instead of micromanaging

Within 3 months, productivity rose and so did team morale. People didn't just follow tasks—they followed her vision.

Reflect & Practice

Ask Yourself:

1. What is my deeper purpose as a leader?
2. Do I lead with ego or with empathy?
3. What decision today requires me to balance compassion with clarity?

Weekly Practice:

- ✓ Begin your Monday by revisiting your leadership purpose.
- ✓ Conduct a "Ram Review" at the week's end: Where did I lead like Ram? Where did I fall short?

Final Thought

Lord Ram never set out to be a king—he became one by serving, uplifting and walking the hard path with dignity. Today, as you build teams, solve problems and face setbacks, remember:

"Leadership is not about power. It is about alignment with purpose and the courage to walk it—even alone."

If you lead with Ram's spirit, people will follow—not just your instructions, but your vision.

Chapter 6

PURPOSE-DRIVEN ACTION — HOW RAM'S CLARITY OF MISSION INSPIRES MODERN LEADERSHIP

"A leader without purpose is a warrior without a target."

In an age of constant notifications, shifting priorities and decision fatigue, clarity of purpose is no longer optional—it is a strategic advantage.

Lord Ram, throughout the Ramayana, stands as a beacon of unwavering purpose. Whether it was honoring his father's word, rescuing Sita, or restoring dharma, Ram never allowed personal ego or emotion to blur his vision. His actions were not reactionary—they were rooted in a deeper mission.

This chapter explores how modern professionals, entrepreneurs and changemakers can unlock purpose-driven performance by learning from Ram's clarity of intent and his ability to act with direction, not distraction.

1. Purpose Before Preference

When Dasharatha ordered Ram's exile, Ram didn't resist, even though it meant giving up his crown. He didn't act out of personal loss. He acted from a higher principle—his duty and his dharma.

Modern Insight: In today's world, many people chase what feels good, not what is good. True leadership and growth come when we choose purpose over preference, mission over mood.

Ask Yourself: Am I driven by convenience or conviction?

2. Mission Anchors Decision-Making

Ram's decisions—from for ming alliances to entering battle—weren't made impulsively. Each one was anchored to his greater goal: to restore righteousness and rescue Sita. He filtered actions through his purpose.

Modern Insight: Without a clear mission, you'll be pulled in 50 directions. Purpose acts as a filter—helping you say no to distractions and yes to what really matters.

Try This: Before every major decision, ask:
"Does this move me closer to my deeper goal?"

3. Leading with Vision, Not Control

Ram led with clarity, not coercion. He inspired Hanuman, Vibhishan and even the tribal communities not by force—but by purpose. He gave people something larger than themselves to be part of.

Modern Insight: Great leaders don't just manage people—they mobilize purpose. Whether you're leading a startup or a student group, clarity of vision draws loyalty and builds momentum.

4. Endurance Requires Purpose

Ram's 14-year exile wasn't just a test of patience—it was a journey that revealed his purpose more deeply. He remained focused, humble and generous even in hardship.

Modern Insight: People often burn out not because they work too hard, but because they work without meaning. Purpose energizes. Without it, even small tasks feel heavy.

Action Step: Write your 1-line "Ram Mindset Purpose Statement" for this phase of your life.

Example:

"To lead with integrity and build a team culture based on trust."

5. Purpose Evolves, But Values Stay Rooted

Ram adapted strategies—from crossing oceans to building alliances—but his core values remained constant: honor, truth and compassion.

Modern Insight: Your methods will change, your roles will shift, but your core principles should be your compass.

Reflection:

What 3 values define your leadership today?

The Ram Purpose Filter – A 3-Step Guide

When making decisions or setting goals, run them through this simple framework:

Step	Filter Question	Purpose Alignment Example
1	Does this serve my higher mission or just my ego?	Building a product to solve a real user problem, not just to impress investors.
2	Will this bring clarity or chaos to my life/team?	Delegating tasks to focus on strategic leadership.

Step	Filter Question	Purpose Alignment Example
3	Is this consistent with my values and vision?	Refusing to compromise on ethical standards.

A Real-World Parallel: The Entrepreneur with a Dharma Lens

Ravi, a young founder, launched a startup to solve mobility challenges in small towns. But when VC pressure pushed him toward urban expansion, he felt lost. After reading about Ram's clarity of purpose, he re-centered his mission.

He said:
"Ram didn't follow power—he followed purpose. That clarity saved me. I pivoted back to what mattered and the business not only grew—it aligned with my values."

Purpose gave Ravi strength—not just to build, but to build what mattered.

Reflect & Practice

Ask Yourself:

- What is my "Why" right now? Is it clear and compelling?
- Am I doing anything today that's misaligned with my deeper mission?
- What would Ram's example inspire me to let go of?

Daily Purpose Practice:

- ✓ Each morning, write your top 3 priorities.
- ✓ For each, ask: "Does this serve my deeper mission?"
- ✓ End your day by noting 1 purposeful action you took.

Final Thought

Ram didn't chase fame, titles, or personal comfort. He followed a deeper calling—to live and lead by values, to serve a cause greater than himself. That's the essence of the Ram Mindset.

"Purpose turns pain into progress and struggle into strategy."
Let Ram's clarity light the way.

Chapter 7

RESILIENCE IN CHAOS — HOW RAM OVERCAME EXILE, LOSS AND WAR WITH GRACE

"In the face of darkness, Ram chose light—not because it was easy, but because it was right."

In today's hyper-competitive, emotionally draining world, resilience isn't optional—it's a core life skill. Whether you're an entrepreneur facing uncertainty, a student grappling with failure, or a working professional dealing with pressure, your ability to bounce back without breaking defines your long-term success.

Few stories in world literature offer a more powerful template for resilience than the life of Lord Ram. Banished from his kingdom, separated from his wife, betrayed by those close to him and burdened with unimaginable responsibilities—Ram endured it all with grace, strength and calm clarity.

In this chapter, we explore how to adopt the Ram Mindset of Resilience—a powerful blend of emotional balance, moral clarity and inner strength—for navigating the storms of modern life.

1. Acceptance: The First Step Toward Strength

When Ram was told he must leave for 14 years of exile, he didn't resist. He didn't argue. He accepted the truth and acted with dignity. This wasn't weakness—it was wisdom.

Modern Insight: Most people waste energy resisting reality. Ram teaches us that resilience begins with acceptance, not avoidance. Acceptance brings focus. Resistance breeds suffering.

Action Practice: Instead of asking "Why me?", ask "What now?"

2. Composure in the Face of Injustice

Ram never responded to unfairness with bitterness. Whether it was Kaikeyi's demand or Ravan's betrayal, Ram stayed calm, anchored in values, not emotions.

Modern Insight: Workplaces and life will never be fair. Emotional reactivity drains your power. Leaders and changemakers must cultivate emotional detachment and moral focus.

Try This: Before reacting, take 3 breaths and ask:
"What would Ram do here?"

3. Purpose-Fueled Endurance

Ram didn't survive exile because of physical strength. He thrived because he saw his journey as part of a larger purpose. Every hardship was an opportunity to embody dharma.

Modern Insight: When life feels hard, connect to why you're doing it. Resilience isn't about blind toughness. It's about remembering what matters and staying aligned.

4. Leading with Empathy in Tough Times

Ram led Vanaras, tribals and allies with compassion. He never used power to dominate, only to uplift. Even in war, he showed empathy and forgiveness (as with Vibhishan and even Ravan at times).

Modern Insight: Leadership during crisis is not about command—it's about calm. Resilient leaders inspire by staying grounded and showing compassion, even under pressure.

5. The Warrior Who Waited

Ram didn't rush into battle. He prepared, planned and waited for the right moment. His resilience was patient, not impulsive.

Modern Insight: When things go wrong, our impulse is to rush, fix, act. But strategic patience is a core trait of resilient professionals and entrepreneurs.

The Ram Resilience Framework

Here's a simple model to follow during any personal or professional storm:

Phase	Ram's Way	Your Practice
Accept	Embrace the truth, don't resist	Journal: "What is true right now?"
Anchor	Stay calm, act from values	Pause. Breathe. Choose the wiser path
Adapt	Change strategy, not purpose	Ask: "What needs to evolve?"
Act	Take focused, value-aligned action	Small wins. One step at a time.
Appreciate	Reflect and stay grateful	End your day with 3 learnings

A Real-World Story: Turning Setback into Strength

Maya, a senior marketing executive, was let go from her job during a company downsizing. For weeks she felt helpless and angry.

After reading about Ram's resilience, she changed her approach. She said:

"I realized I was stuck in blame mode. Ram didn't do that. He focused on purpose. So I did too. I built my personal brand online, helped others and found a better opportunity within 3 months."

Maya didn't bounce back by accident. She chose purposeful resilience, Ram-style.

Reflect & Practice

Ask Yourself:

- What recent challenge have I not fully accepted?
- How can I anchor myself when things feel unfair?
- What long-term purpose will carry me through today's difficulty?

Try This Weekly Practice:

1. Storm Scan: Write down your 3 biggest stressors.
2. For each, ask:
   - What can I accept?
   - What can I control?
   - What can I release?
3. Choose 1 daily action from a place of calm, not chaos.

Final Thought

Ram's greatness was not just in his victories—but in his ability to rise with dignity after every fall, betrayal, or loss. Resilience isn't about being unbreakable. It's about staying whole when life breaks around you.

“The Ram Mindset is not about escaping adversity, but embodying grace within it.”

Chapter 8

PURPOSE AND PATIENCE — WALKING THE LONG ROAD WITH GRACE

"A journey with purpose can bear any pause. A life without it collapses at the first delay."

In a world addicted to speed, Lord Ram's journey is a powerful contrast. Fourteen years in exile. Thirteen years in search. And still, not a moment wasted in resentment or restlessness.
Ram didn't just walk a forest path — he walked a life path with unshakable purpose and the patience to honor it.

Today, professionals are under pressure to "make it" fast. Careers must soar. Results must be instant. But purpose isn't microwaved. It's cultivated — with time, clarity and inner steadiness.

This chapter helps you build a mindset that walks long roads without burning out — just like Ram did.

1. Purpose Is the Compass — Not the Clock

Ram never complained about exile because he didn't see it as a delay — he saw it as part of the duty. His goal wasn't a throne — it was righteousness.

Modern Insight: When you attach your identity to purpose, not position, setbacks stop feeling like failures.

Example:
You're not "just" a junior executive — you're someone learning to become a value-driven leader.
You're not "still" a startup — you're building something that serves real people with honesty.

2. The Myth of Overnight Success

The Ramayana spans decades — not days. Even divine missions unfolded with patience, step-by-step.
Today, we see highlight reels on LinkedIn and Instagram and mistake them for real-life timelines.

Modern Insight: Real purpose is invisible for long stretches — but never lost.

Try This: Write down:

- Your 5-year purpose
- Your 1-year progress goals
- One tiny thing you can do today that aligns with both

3. Delays Are Not Denials

Ram could have questioned the fairness of his exile. But instead, he used the forest as a space for reflection, alliance-building and skill-building.

Modern Insight: Life's "waiting rooms" are often where character is built. Don't waste them.

Ask Yourself:

- What is this delay trying to teach me?
- How can I grow while I wait?

4. Slow Growth, Strong Roots

The trees of Panchavati didn't grow in a day — and neither did Ram's legend. His calm, his strategy, his alliances, his battles — all unfolded in phases.
In the same way, a strong life isn't built in a viral moment—it's shaped through quiet, steady growth.

Modern Insight: Don't rush the becoming. Trust the becoming.

5. **Purpose Makes You Resilient**

Ram's purpose wasn't reactive — it was rooted. That's why no exile, no storm, no criticism could shake him.
Purpose isn't just a vision. It's a shield against chaos and a bridge across difficulty.

Modern Analogy: A startup with clear mission survives market dips. A professional with deep purpose survives office politics. A parent with values survives exhaustion.

Modern Tools for Purpose + Patience

Here are 3 ways to embody Ram's mindset in your daily hustle:

1. **Purpose Journal (5 minutes/week)**

Reflect on:

- “What did I do this week that aligned with my purpose?”
- “What distracted me?”
- “What will I focus on next week?”

2. **Delay Gratitude Practice**

Instead of dreading what's slow, thank it. Write 3 benefits of this current “waiting phase” in your life.

3. **Vision > Victories**

Create a vision board for 5 years ahead. Pin it where you work. It's your North Star — not your to-do list.

Final Thought

Ram's greatness didn't come from speed. It came from steadiness. He kept walking. Kept believing. Kept growing. And so can you. Your purpose is not a race to finish. It's a rhythm to follow. A fire to keep warm — not burn out.

"Hold your vision. Honor your pace. Trust the path — even when it disappears under your feet."

Chapter 9

MODERN-DAY VANVAS: HANDLING CAREER SETBACKS, REJECTIONS & TRANSITIONS

"Sometimes life forces you away from comfort so you can discover who you truly are."

Ram's vanvas (exile) wasn't a punishment —it was preparation.

A prince accustomed to comfort suddenly found himself in the forest, stripped of luxury, status, and privilege. Yet he did not complain, panic, or lose clarity of purpose.

Vanvas is not a place — it is a phase.

A transition where life tests whether you can still walk your path when everything is taken away.

Modern professionals face their own vanvas:

- Losing a job
- Being rejected for promotion
- Startup failure
- Relocation to a new city
- Unexpected career breaks
- Feeling undervalued despite strong efforts

Instead of questioning "Why me?", Ram teaches us to ask:
"What is life preparing me for?"

The Mindset Shift: Forest to Opportunity

Ram's Vanvas	Modern Experience	What It Teaches
Leaving the palace	Losing career comfort	Growth begins when comfort ends

Ram's Vanvas	Modern Experience	What It Teaches
Less resources, more responsibility	Handling pressure with limited support	Creativity & resilience are developed in scarcity
Staying focused despite injustice	Unfair treatment at work	Choose discipline over drama
Serving people in the forest	Doing lesser-known roles	Leadership begins without titles

Ram didn't wait for the throne to act like a king — He continued to lead wherever he stood.

Rejection as Redirection

Kaikeyi's demand pushed Ram away from Ayodhya but closer to:

- Meeting Hanuman
- Building alliances
- Eliminating adharmic rule
- Establishing Ram Rajya

Your setbacks may also be setting up:

- A better opportunity
- Right mentors and supporters
- A stronger version of you
- A purpose-led direction

The door that closes is not the end — It's the corridor to the door meant for you.

Emotional Lessons from Vanvas

Ram didn't allow:

- Fear to block progress
- Anger to cloud judgment
- Sadness to define identity

He practiced:

- Acceptance
- Adaptability
- Inner calm
- Purpose over ego

This is the Ram Mindset for every professional stuck in uncertainty.

Strategy for Your Vanvas Phase

Step 1 — Accept Reality, Without Victim Mindset
Say: "This is my training phase."

Step 2 — Upgrade Skills
Use downtime to grow professionally.

Step 3 — Rebuild Your Support Army
Ram met Hanuman in the forest —
Your network may strengthen too.

Step 4 — Stay Loyal to Your Purpose
Even without the title — be the leader.

Reflection Questions

Ask yourself:

1. What am I learning that comfort would never teach me?
2. Who is entering my life during this transition?
3. What future success is this preparing me for?

Transitions transform ordinary individuals into heroes of their own story.

Message for us

"You don't become Ram in Ayodhya. You become Ram in the forest."

Your modern-day vanvas is not punishment —It is the path to purpose.

Welcome it. Walk through it and rise from it stronger than ever.

Chapter 10

SITA'S STRENGTH — EMOTIONAL RESILIENCE, DIGNITY AND PATIENCE IN UNFAIR TIMES

"True strength is not loud. It endures, it forgives and it rises — again and again."

— Inspired by the endurance of Sita

Introduction: The Quiet Power of Grace Under Pressure

In the Ramayana, Sita is often perceived through the lens of her suffering — exile, abduction, trials by fire. But to view her only as a victim is to miss her extraordinary emotional intelligence, inner strength and moral courage.

In this chapter, we explore how Sita's mental resilience, unwavering dignity and calm decision-making provide powerful lessons for professionals, students and anyone navigating unfair, stressful, or emotionally charged environments.

1. Grace in Adversity

Sita's strength was not physical, but mental and emotional. In moments when she could've reacted with anger, she chose composure. In situations beyond her control, she chose to respond, not react.

Modern Insight: Not everything in your career or relationships will be fair — but your response defines your power.

Try This: Before reacting in a tough conversation, ask yourself:

- "Am I choosing dignity or defense?"
- "How would Sita handle this — with poise or panic?"

2. Dignity Over Drama

Even when doubted or challenged, Sita never begged for validation.

She let her actions and integrity speak for her.

Modern Insight: When you face criticism, don't rush to justify. Lead with your values, not your voice.

Self-Coaching Tip:

- List 3 values you want to embody at work or in relationships.
- In moments of tension, return to this list. Respond from strength, not ego.

3. Sita's Boundaries: Compassion, Not Compliance

Sita went to the forest out of love, not weakness. She chose to accompany Ram — not because she was told to, but because she chose to stand beside him.

Modern Insight: There's a difference between sacrifice with self-respect and compliance out of fear. Sita teaches us to set boundaries, even while being loving and loyal.

Ask Yourself:

- "Am I choosing this path from strength or fear?"
- "Does this align with my dignity?"

4. Silence is Sometimes Strategy

In Ashok Vatika, surrounded by enemies, Sita kept her silence. She knew when to speak — and more importantly, when not to.

Modern Insight: Silence is not weakness. It is often awareness, observation and preservation.

Situational Insight: In toxic meetings or emotionally charged moments, silence can be more powerful than argument.

5. The Fire Within

The Agni Pariksha (trial by fire) is often misinterpreted. Beyond the literal, it symbolizes Sita's ability to walk through the fire of judgment — and emerge pure, not just in body, but in character.

Modern Insight: Every professional will face a “trial by fire” — layoffs, blame, self-doubt. Let it forge you, not break you.

Mental Frame: “Every fire I walk through will burn my fear, not my worth.”

6. Forgiveness Is Not Forgetting — It's Freedom

Even after facing rejection and exile while pregnant, Sita never expressed vengeance. Her forgiveness wasn't passive; it was freeing.

Modern Insight: Carrying resentment consumes mental energy. Forgiveness, when chosen with awareness, releases that weight — not for others, but for your own peace.

7. Leaving With Self-Respect

Sita's final decision — to return to Mother Earth — was not surrender. It was sovereignty. She had said and done enough. She chose closure with clarity, not continued suffering.

Modern Insight: In work or relationships, know when your part is done. Know when to walk away — with dignity, not defeat.

The "Sita Strength" Framework

Quality	Modern Interpretation
Emotional Balance	Pause before reacting; channel strength inward
Dignity	Let actions speak louder than defense
Forgiveness	Don't let bitterness block your clarity
Boundaries	Sacrifice only when it honors your self-worth
Closure	Exit situations with clarity and grace

Final Reflection: Not All Power Wears Armor

Sita's power wasn't in weapons or warfare. It was in emotional steadiness, mental resilience and the ability to hold onto her truth without losing her grace.

"In a world that celebrates noise, be like Sita — strong, silent and deeply rooted in your worth."

Chapter 11

RAVAN'S MIND PSYCHOLOGY — WHAT AMBITION WITHOUT DHARMA LEADS TO

11. Ravan's Mind Psychology — What Ambition Without Dharma Leads To

Overview

Ravan was one of the most intelligent, powerful, and learned rulers in history — a master of the Vedas, an unmatched strategist, and a king of prosperity.

Yet, his legacy is defined by self-destruction, not success.

Why?

Because ambition without dharma becomes ego.
And ego left unchecked becomes a leader's downfall.

This chapter explores the psychology behind Ravan's choices — and reflects how modern leaders and individuals can avoid the same trap.

Key Sections & Insights

1. The Genius of Ravan — Strengths Every Leader Should Learn

Ravan possessed qualities that can inspire:

- Supreme confidence
- Brilliance in statecraft & warfare
- Mastery of knowledge
- Fearless pursuit of goals

Leadership Insight:

Ambition is a superpower — when aligned with moral purpose.

2. The First Crack: Ego Masquerading as Self-Respect

Ravan demanded respect instead of earning it.

He believed:
"If I am great, everyone must obey me."
But true leaders know:
Respect flows from actions, not authority.

Lesson: A great leader influences, a tyrant enforces.

3. Attachment to Desire — The Fall Begins

Ravan's obsession with Sita was not love — it was desire, control, and superiority.
He believed: "If I want something, I deserve it."

Leadership Insight:
Ambition driven by greed hijacks wisdom — and blinds judgment.

4. Surrounding Himself With Yes-Men

Ravan rejected wise advice from:

- Vibhishan — dharma-driven brother
- Mandodari — wise and emotionally grounded queen

He silenced voices of truth and rewarded flattery instead.

Lesson:
A leader who fears criticism invites defeat.
The moment a leader believes "I am always right," collapse begins.

5. Power Without Accountability

Ravan saw rules as obstacles — not principles.
Consequences?

- Arrogance replaced discipline
- Emotion overshadowed intelligence
- Decision-making was driven by personal validation

Leadership Insight: Power is safe only when governed by ethics.

6. The Psychology of Downfall

Ravan's leadership suffered from three internal enemies:
Lesson:

Internal Enemy	**How It Appeared**	**Impact on Leadership**
Ego (Ahamkar)	Disregarding advice	Clouded judgment
Attachment (Moha)	Desire for Sita	War without strategy
Anger (Krodha)	Impulsive revenge	Destruction of Lanka

When emotions rule a leader, chaos rules the kingdom.

Modern Leadership Reflection

Ravan is present in today's workplaces when:

- Leaders prioritize position over purpose
- Feedback is viewed as threat
- Winning matters more than doing what's right
- Personal desire replaces team welfare

Self-Check for Leaders:

- Do I welcome honest disagreement?
- Are my goals aligned with values?
- Does my growth help others grow?

If the answer is no — Ravan's shadow is forming.

Final Thought

The Final Lesson of Ravan's Mind -Ravan stands as a timeless reminder:

Greatness without humility collapses.
Success without values is failure.
Ambition without dharma leads to destruction.

To lead like Ram, learn from Ravan:

- Have dreams, but stay grounded
- Chase excellence, not domination
- Hold power, but not pride

When dharma guides ambition —
power transforms into legacy, not ruin.

Chapter 12

THE POWER OF RELATIONSHIPS — BUILDING TRUST, LOYALTY AND SUPPORT LIKE RAM

"True leadership is not about commanding followers, but cultivating relationships built on loyalty, mutual respect and shared purpose."

In today's fast-paced world, people feel more connected digitally yet more disconnected emotionally than ever before. Professional relationships are often transactional. Friendships are fleeting. And trust—once broken—is hard to repair.

But the life of Lord Ram, as depicted in the Ramayana, offers enduring lessons on the art of building and sustaining meaningful relationships.

From his unshakable bond with Lakshman and Hanuman to the grace he extended to allies and adversaries alike, Ram's relationships were based on trust, empathy, purpose and sacrifice.

In this chapter, we'll explore actionable insights from Ram's relational leadership to help today's professionals, entrepreneurs and changemakers nurture powerful human bonds in work and life.

1. Trust Is the Foundation

Ram trusted Lakshman to walk beside him in exile, Bharat to rule Ayodhya in his absence and Hanuman to carry out critical missions. He never micromanaged—he empowered with belief.

Modern Insight: Great leaders trust others to lead. They delegate with clarity and faith, not fear.

Practical Step:
Start one trust-based delegation at work this week. Let go of control and allow ownership.

2. Loyalty Is Earned Through Integrity

Hanuman's loyalty wasn't demanded—it was earned. Through humility, consistency and alignment with dharma, Ram inspired devotion.

Modern Insight: Loyalty isn't a demand—it's a natural result of values-aligned behavior. Show up with authenticity and fairness, even when no one is watching.

Ask Yourself:
"Am I consistent in how I treat people across roles, ranks and circumstances?"

3. The Power of Listening

When Vibhishan, Ravana's own brother, defected to Ram's side, Ram didn't dismiss him. He listened with openness, gave him space to speak and embraced his sincerity.

Modern Insight: Listening is leadership. Whether you manage a team or run a home, listening fosters belonging and diffuses conflict.

Try This: In your next conversation, don't interrupt. Ask a follow-up question instead of offering advice.

4. Purpose Bonds Relationships

Ram's relationships were mission-driven. Hanuman, Sugriv and even the Vanar Sena followed him not just out of affection, but because they believed in his purpose.

Modern Insight: In workplaces and startups, purpose attracts commitment. When people believe in the "why," they walk with you through storms.

Leadership Prompt:
"Have I clearly communicated why this work matters?"

5. **Letting Go with Love**

One of the hardest decisions Ram made was to ask Sita to leave Ayodhya due to public perception, despite his deep love. It was not rejection—it was responsibility.

Modern Insight: Sometimes, leadership and relationships demand emotionally painful but principled decisions. Choosing the greater good may require letting go with grace.

Reflection Question:
"Where am I holding on out of attachment, not alignment?"

Ram's Relationship Blueprint – The 5 Elements of Enduring Bonds

Element	Ram's Example	Modern Application
Trust	Letting Lakshman lead in war zones	Delegate with belief, not fear
Loyalty	Earning Hanuman's devotion	Be consistent in values
Listening	Welcoming Vibhishan with an open heart	Create space for others' truths

Element	Ram's Example	Modern Application
Shared Purpose	Rallying allies to rescue Sita	Align teams around a mission
Emotional Grace	Letting Sita go while holding love	Choose clarity over comfort when needed

Real-World Parallel: Building a "Ram Team" Culture

Ravi, a senior project manager in a global IT firm, realized his team was burning out and emotionally disengaged. He paused the sprint one week to host a simple "Ram Circle" inspired check-in:

- What are you struggling with (emotionally or professionally)?
- Where do you need trust or support?
- How can we show up better as a team?

The shift was immediate. Silence gave way to sharing. People reconnected. Ownership increased. Within 3 weeks, team productivity and emotional bonding improved.

"I stopped managing the work. I started managing the relationships," Ravi reflected.

Daily Practice: Nurturing "Ram-Style" Relationships

- ✓ Morning Intention: Choose one person to truly listen to today.
- ✓ Midday Reflection: Acknowledge one act of loyalty or trust from someone.
- ✓ Night Note: Send a message of appreciation to someone who stood by you.

Final Thought

Lord Ram teaches us that relationships are not built on charisma—but on character. Through empathy, trust and shared purpose, he created bonds that didn't just help him succeed—they helped him lead with grace.

“A king's true strength lies not in his army, but in the hearts of those who willingly follow him”

Chapter 13

RAM RAJYA WITHIN — LEADING TEAMS WITH FAIRNESS, EMPATHY AND STRENGTH

"Leadership is not about commanding the land — it's about serving its people with justice and care."

— Inspired by the ideals of Ram Rajya

Introduction: What Is Ram Rajya?

Ram Rajya is more than an ancient ideal — it's a timeless blueprint for leadership that balances justice, empathy, vision and service. In the Ramayana, Lord Ram doesn't rule to dominate. He rules to elevate.

Today, whether you're a team lead, entrepreneur, manager, or even a parent — your version of Ram Rajya starts with how you lead those around you.

This chapter translates the ethics of Ram's leadership into modern, actionable strategies for professionals and changemakers.

1. Justice Without Bias — Fairness Builds Trust

Lord Ram was known for upholding Dharma even when it came at personal cost. His decisions weren't about pleasing everyone — they were about doing what was right for the greater good.

Modern Insight: A leader's credibility comes not from being agreeable, but from being consistently fair.

Example:
Avoid favouritism in performance reviews. Set transparent expectations. Explain tough decisions respectfully.

2. Empathy Over Ego — Listening Is Leadership

Ram always listened — to sages, villagers, even adversaries. His ability to understand before acting made him a trusted king and a compassionate leader.

Modern Insight: Great leaders listen deeply before they speak. They ask, "What does this person need?" not just "What should they do?"

Try This: In your next one-on-one, ask:

- "What's been challenging for you this week?"
- "How can I support you better?"

3. Leading with Integrity — The Inside Reflects the Outside

When Ram sent Sita to the forest, he didn't do it out of personal doubt — but to preserve the trust of the people. It was an incredibly painful but selfless act made from his duty as king, not his emotions as a husband.

Modern Insight: Sometimes, leadership requires sacrifice — not to serve ego, but to serve a mission.

Note: Modern readers must understand this episode in its full context and symbolism — not as gender-based judgment, but as a test of the complexity of public leadership.

4. Inclusiveness — Empowering All Stakeholders

Ram built alliances across caste, species and geography — from Hanuman (a Vanara) to Vibhishan (a Rakshasa). He saw value in character, not labels.

Modern Insight: True leaders build diverse teams — they include those with integrity and potential, regardless of background.

Actionable Tip: Hire for values, not just resumes. Promote based on impact, not just visibility.

5. Balance Strength with Sensitivity

Ram was a warrior — yet deeply emotional. He grieved, reflected, forgave and celebrated with humility.

Modern Insight: Vulnerability doesn't weaken leadership — it humanizes it.

Try This: Share one personal challenge with your team that taught you something. It builds trust and relatability.

Leadership Toolkit: Ram Rajya for Modern Leaders

Principle	**Practice Example**
Fairness	Define and share decision-making criteria
Empathy	Active listening in team meetings
Integrity	Walk the talk — your team is watching
Inclusion	Create space for diverse voices and feedback
Strength + Sensitivity	Address conflict calmly but firmly

The Inner Ram Rajya: Self-Leadership First

Before leading others, Ram led himself — with restraint, wisdom and self-discipline.

Modern Insight: Your team reflects your energy. If you want clarity and calm in your team — cultivate it within.

Reflection Journal Prompt:

- "Where am I being reactive instead of responsive?"
- "How can I model what I expect from others?"

Final Thought

Ram Rajya isn't about being perfect — it's about being principled.

To lead like Ram in today's world doesn't require a crown or a kingdom.

It requires:

✓ Clarity of intention
✓ Consistency of action
✓ Compassion in communication

"Lead not to be followed — lead to elevate others. That is the Ram Mindset."

Chapter 14

LAKSHMAN'S LOYALTY — COMMITMENT AND BOUNDARIES IN LEADERSHIP

"commitment is not just staying—it is standing with purpose."

Lakshman, the younger brother of Lord Ram, is often remembered as the embodiment of unwavering loyalty and protection. He left behind comfort, a royal life, and even his own personal boundaries to support Ram during the years of vanvas (exile).

In modern leadership, the principles behind Lakshman's loyalty hold a powerful message: dedication is admirable—but it must be aligned with purpose, balance, and self-respect.

1. Loyalty as a Leadership Strength

Loyalty builds trust — the strongest foundation of any relationship, team, or organization.

- Lakshman followed Ram not out of obligation, but conviction.
- His actions showed loyalty to a person and to the ideal of dharma.
- True loyalty fuels courage during adversity.

Modern Lesson

Great team players do not just follow instructions; they stand for the mission and the leader's integrity.

Be loyal to values, not positions.

2. Dedication Requires Sacrifice — But Not Self-Destruction

During exile, Lakshman stayed awake for 14 years, guarding Ram and Sita without rest.

This extreme sacrifice teaches two sides of leadership:

- Commitment can unlock superhuman ability.
- Overcommitment can cost personal well-being

Many professionals today:

- Work late nights
- Sacrifice emotional balance
- Burn out chasing success

Modern Lesson

A leader should encourage commitment with boundaries, not blind sacrifice.

3. Healthy Boundaries Support Healthy Loyalty

Lakshman drew the famous Lakshman Rekha—a symbol of:

- Protection
- Awareness
- Respect for space

Boundaries are essential in teams:

- Setting limits prevents emotional exploitation
- Saying "no" protects professional focus
- Empathy must not override self-respect

Boundaries are not barriers — they are the structure that keeps relationships strong.

4. The Balance Between Protecting Others and Protecting Self

Lakshman always prioritized Ram's mission before his own needs. But during war, especially against Indrajit, we see a different dimension:

He knows when:

- To step forward as a defender
- To step back and heal when injured

Modern Lesson: Effective leaders
and team members:

- Help others succeed
- But do not destroy their own ability to contribute

Self-care is not selfish. It is responsibility.

5. Courage to Challenge Wrong — Even in Relationships

Loyalty does not mean blind acceptance.
Lakshman questioned decisions when needed (like during Sita's exile).

He lived by a rule:

Support the person, challenge the wrong.

Modern Lesson

Organizations progress when team members:

- Raise ethical concerns
- Speak truth respectfully
- Protect values even if it risks approval

6. Action Steps — Adopting the Lakshman Leadership Code

Lakshman Principle	Modern Action	Result
Loyalty to dharma	Align with mission and values	Strong trust & unity
Boundary discipline	Clear expectations & limits	Healthy team dynamics
Stand firm in crises	Stay calm during pressure	Respect & credibility
Courage to question	Give constructive feedback	Ethical culture
Balanced sacrifice	Protect your mental health	Sustainable performance

A Reflection Exercise

Ask yourself:

- What or who am I loyal to — the person, or the principle?
- Do I draw a "Lakshman Rekha" around my mental and physical boundaries?
- Does my dedication support my growth or exhaust me?
- Can I challenge leadership while still supporting the mission?

Write 3 changes you can make starting this week to practice responsible loyalty.

Final Thought

Lakshman teaches us that loyalty is most powerful when rooted in dignity:

Loyalty should not make you smaller. It should make the mission stronger.

Following his example, we learn to:

- Commit with passion
- Protect our boundaries
- Support with wisdom
- Lead with courage

This is the essence of Loyalty with Leadership Intelligence — a value every modern professional must embrace.

Chapter 15

BHARATA'S SACRIFICE: SELFLESS LEADERSHIP & ZERO-EGO MANAGEMENT

*"True leadership isn't about the throne you sit on —
it's about the values you stand for."*

When we think of Ramayana, Shri Ram stands as the embodiment of dharma. But right beside him is Bharata, whose story is one of the most powerful examples of selfless leadership in human history.

While Ram was exiled, Bharata was offered the kingdom — a position most would desire. Yet Bharata rejected power that did not align with dharma. He put values above authority, relationships above personal gain.

His sacrifice teaches us a crucial rule of The Ram Mindset:
Leadership is not a privilege — it is a responsibility.

The Crown Without Ego
Bharata had the perfect chance to take the throne:

- No one could question him
- It was his mother's demand
- The kingdom needed a leader

Yet his response was revolutionary —
"I will rule only in Ram's name, not my own."

Instead of sitting on a royal throne, Bharata placed Ram's footwear (Paduka) on it and ruled as a caretaker. That act symbolizes:

- Zero-ego leadership
- Stewardship over ownership
- Loyalty over authority

- Purpose over position

Modern leaders often chase:

- Designations
- Benefits
- Spotlight

But Bharata reminds us: Leadership is not about "being the king"— It's about "serving like a guardian."

Lessons for Today's Professionals

Bharata's Principle	**Modern Application**
Serve the mission, not the ego	Let decisions benefit the organization, not personal brand
Respect rightful authority	Empower team leads and decision-makers
Walk the path of integrity even when unseen	Build trust: do the right things even off the record
Be loyal to purpose, not position	Your growth follows your contribution
Lead with humility	Celebrate team wins more than your own

In today's corporate world, one silent killer of culture is ego:

- "My idea must win."
- "My credit must be recognized."
- "My promotion is the priority."

Bharata shows us how a team transforms when ego disappears.

Bharata-Style Leadership Habits
Here are simple practices to adopt in daily work:

Habit	**Impact**
Step back and allow others to shine	Builds leadership pipeline
Credit others publicly, take accountability privately	Creates trust
Treat every role as service to mission	Increases fulfillment
Consult team before acting	Enhances collaboration
Decline recognition you did not earn	Preserves integrity

Ask yourself:

"Do I want to be important or do I want to do something important?"

Self-Reflection Exercise

Take a moment to reflect on these questions:

- Do I chase power or purpose?
- Do I serve or do I expect to be served?
- How often do I give up my ego for the team?

Write a simple commitment:
"I will lead to uplift others, not to elevate myself."

The Bharata Mindset — Zero-Ego Management

A truly great leader does not create followers —They create more leaders.

And that is exactly what Bharata did:

- He guarded the kingdom not as a ruler…
- But as a trustee…

This chapter calls you to adopt the same:

- Lead with humility
- Serve with loyalty
- Act with integrity
- Put purpose above power

Message for us

Authority can be gifted.
Respect must be earned.
And legacy is built through selfless leadership.

Become a leader who —Not only wears the crown, but protects the values it stands for.

Chapter 16

PARENTS AS LEADERS: KING DASHRATH, KAUSHALYA & THE FAMILY DHARMA SYSTEM

"A strong society is built on strong families and strong families are led with love, values, and responsibility."

Before Shri Ram became a symbol of ideal leadership, discipline, and character — he learned it at home.

King Dashrath, Queen Kaushalya, and the family dharma structure played a foundational role in shaping Ram's greatness.
Their leadership wasn't limited to a royal throne —They led by example, not authority.

Family as the First School of Leadership. From childhood, Ram was taught:

- Compassion from Kaushalya.
- Duty from Dashrath.
- Resilience from the family's challenges.
- Emotional maturity by observing relationships within the palace

Parents often underestimate the power of their behavior. Children rarely follow advice —They mirror character, habits, integrity, and consistency they witness daily.

Dashrath — Leadership with Deep Love but Vulnerable to Emotional Weakness

King Dashrath ruled with fairness and devotion, teaching:

- Justice must never be compromised.
- Decisions must uphold dharma.
- Leadership means being accountable to people

But his emotional attachment led to:

- An impulsive decision to honor a promise.
- Sacrificing Ram for Kaikeyi's demand

Lesson for modern parents:
Love must guide decisions — but wisdom must govern them.

Kaushalya — Graceful Strength & Emotional Stability

Queen Kaushalya showcased:

- Patience during injustice.
- Unconditional love.
- Emotional balance during crisis

She didn't protest loudly — Her calm strength shaped Ram's internal stability.

Lesson:
The tone you set at home becomes the voice inside your child's mind.

Kaikeyi — Love Misguided by Influence

Kaikeyi was not evil — she was misled by toxic persuasion.
Her arc teaches parents:

- Don't allow external influence to control family decisions.
- Avoid favoritism — it destroys trust.
- Decisions must be fair even when emotionally difficult

Modern reflection:
A small ego-driven decision can break lifelong relationships.

Lessons for Today's Parents & Leaders

Family Dharma Principle	Application in Modern Parenting
Lead by living your values	Be the example you want children to follow
Discipline with love, not fear	Correct behaviors without crushing confidence
Stay united as parents	Differences should stay private, not affect kids
Prioritize emotional security	Celebrate effort, not just achievements
Teach purpose, not just performance	Help children build inner strength & meaning

Parents are CEOs of the household—but their success is measured by:
The character they build, not the comfort they provide.

Family Policies = Dharma System Just like a kingdom needs rules—so does a family.
Create a home environment where:

- Respect is non-negotiable.
- Truth is rewarded.
- Gratitude is practiced.
- Service and empathy are taught as daily habits

This becomes the Family Dharma System.

Self-Reflection — Are We Raising Rams or Ravanas?

Ask:

- Are we teaching humility and responsibility?
- Are we rewarding ego or effort?
- Are we showing our children how to handle failures gracefully?

Every "future leader" first learns self-control, respect, and purpose at home.

The Parental Leadership Mindset
"The greatest inheritance you can give your children
is strength of character."

A parent's role is not to build the path for a child — but to build the child for the path.

Message for us

Parenting isn't a role.
It is leadership — where the impact goes far beyond one lifetime.
Like Dashrath and Kaushalya shaped Ram —Every parent is shaping the future through the children they raise.

Chapter 17

THE MENTOR MINDSET: WISDOM FROM VASHISHTHA & VISHWAMITRA

"The right mentor doesn't just teach — they transform you."

Before Ram became the ideal leader, warrior, and king —he first became the ideal student.

Two guiding forces shaped his journey:

- Guru Vashishtha — Master of inner discipline, dharma & emotional stability
- Guru Vishwamitra — Master of warfare, strategy & real-world challenges

These two mentors represent the two essential dimensions of success:

- Vashishtha builds the character.
- Vishwamitra builds the capability.

Both are needed for a leader to rise.

Lesson 1: Internal Strength Comes First — From Guru Vashishtha

Before teaching weapons, Vashishtha taught:

- Self-control over impulses
- Humility despite royalty
- Service before authority
- Clear thinking under pressure

This is the mindset mastery that professions demand today:

- Hold emotional balance during conflict

- Lead without ego
- Choose ethics even when shortcuts tempt you
- Stay grounded with success

Leadership begins within.

Lesson 2: The World Will Test You — Training from Guru Vishwamitra

Vishwamitra exposed Ram to:

- Threats
- Difficult terrains
- High-stakes missions
- Real battlefield pressure

He taught Ram:

- Courage
- Strategic action
- Crisis management
- Quick decision-making

Just like organizations do today:

- New roles = new challenges
- Bigger leadership = bigger battles
- Growth = discomfort

A mentor prepares you for life beyond the classroom.

Two Mentors. One Heroic Outcome.

Mentor	**Teachings**	**Modern Professional Parallel**
Vashishtha	Dharma, inner peace, wisdom	Emotional intelligence, character development
Vishwamitra	Skills, strategy, fearlessness	Performance excellence, innovation

Both played a role in shaping Ram's balanced leadership —

- Compassion + Competence
- Spirituality + Strategy
- Heart + Mind

Your Mentor Mindset

To succeed like Ram, build a circle of mentors:

- Personal Mentor (Values, confidence, clarity) — Like Vashishtha
- Professional Mentor (Skills, strategy, execution)— Like Vishwamitra

A single mentor cannot teach everything. Growth demands multiple perspectives. Seek mentors who challenge your limitations, not those who compliment your comfort.

How to Attract Right Mentors

- Be hungry to learn
- Show initiative

- Be humble enough to accept feedback
- Offer value in return, even small
- Stay consistent in effort

When the student is dedicated—the right mentor always arrives.

Reflection Questions

1. Who is shaping your inner discipline today?
2. Who is sharpening your professional edge?
3. What mentorship gap is slowing down your growth?
4. How can you seek and serve mentors better?

Message for us

"Ram did not become Ram alone.
Growth is a team sport.
Mentors are the unseen architects of greatness."

Build yourself like Ram — with the guidance of both a Vashishtha and a Vishwamitra within your life

Chapter 18

LESSONS FROM HANUMAN — THE POWER OF DEVOTION, HUMILITY AND RELENTLESS ACTION

"When your cause is selfless and your heart is pure, nothing is impossible."

— Inspired by the devotion of Hanuman

Introduction: The Unsung Hero of Purposeful Action

While Lord Ram exemplifies moral leadership, Hanuman is the embodiment of dedicated service, unstoppable energy and unshakable humility. His life is not just devotional — it's deeply strategic and action-driven.

In this chapter, we draw timeless lessons from Hanuman's character to empower professionals, students and leaders to take purposeful action — without ego, without burnout and with full integrity.

1. Self-Belief with Humility

Hanuman initially forgot his powers — until reminded by Jambavan. Once awakened, he didn't boast; he acted.

Modern Insight: Most people don't lack skills — they lack the belief that they can act. But belief without ego is what sets true performers apart.

Action Tip: When you doubt yourself, ask:

- "Am I underestimating what I already know?"
- "What would Hanuman do — pause or leap?"

2. Devotion to a Higher Purpose

Hanuman's devotion wasn't blind. It was aligned with a cause: serving Ram's mission and helping others.

Modern Insight: Your best energy comes when you align with a purpose beyond personal gain.

Example:
If you're a team lead, focus on making your team succeed — not just your own metrics. The growth you enable will define your legacy.

3. Energy That Serves, Not Scatters

Hanuman had unmatched energy, but he channelled it with focus and discipline.

Modern Insight: In an age of burnout and distraction, Hanuman teaches us to be energized yet grounded.

Try This: Set "energy check-ins" — short pauses during the day to ask:

- "Am I reacting or responding?"
- "Am I still aligned with my goal or just busy?"

4. Fearless, But Not Reckless

From flying across the ocean to setting Lanka ablaze, Hanuman took bold actions — but always with clarity, not chaos.

Modern Insight: Courage isn't about constant hustle. It's about choosing bold action after reflection.

Leadership Reminder: Before sending that harsh email or making a drastic decision, breathe like Hanuman would — with intention and mission in mind.

5. No Task Too Small

Whether delivering Ram's ring or carrying a mountain, Hanuman gave the same 100%.

Modern Insight: True professionals don't measure a task's importance by visibility — they measure it by impact and service.

Ask Yourself:

- "What task am I treating as 'small' that deserves my full focus?"
- "How would Hanuman approach this?"

6. Hanuman's Productivity Secret: Bhakti + Buddhi

Hanuman combined two superpowers:

- **Bhakti (devotion) → Heart-led work**
- **Buddhi (intellect) → Smart decisions**

Modern Insight: The best work is not just passionate — it's also precise.

Practical Framework (The Hanuman Method):

Element	**Meaning**	**Application**
Bhakti	Selfless commitment	Work for the cause, not the credit
Buddhi	Strategic thinking	Prioritize, plan and pivot when needed
Bal	Energy with intention	Use strength wisely — avoid burnout

Hanuman in the Workplace

Trait	Modern Application
Loyalty	Stick with your team in tough times
Initiative	Don't wait to be asked — offer solutions
Emotional Control	Stay calm even under pressure
Focus	Complete one task at a time, with full effort
Gratitude	Celebrate your team's wins, not just yours

Final Thought: Be the Hanuman of Your Circle

You don't need wings to fly, a tail to fight, or a mountain to lift. You need:

- Devotion to a purpose
- Focused energy
- Humility in victory
- Courage in adversity

"In every workplace, family, or community, there's someone silently holding things together with heart and strength. Be that Hanuman."

Chapter 19

RAM RAJYA — CREATING HARMONY IN TEAMS, FAMILIES AND COMMUNITIES

"True leadership is not about control; it is about creating a world where others can thrive."

— Inspired by Ram Rajya

Introduction: What Was Ram Rajya?

Ram Rajya wasn't just a golden age or utopian dream. It was a value-driven governance model — rooted in justice, inclusion, responsibility and harmony. Lord Ram's rule wasn't admired for wealth or conquest alone, but because every citizen felt heard, safe and respected.

In modern times, "Ram Rajya" is a metaphor for ethical leadership and collective well-being — whether in organizations, homes, or communities.

This chapter explores how you can apply the spirit of Ram Rajya to:

- Lead with values
- Build trust in teams
- Nurture inclusion and fairness
- Create calm, resilient environments

1. Leadership by Listening

Ram took time to understand even the smallest concerns of his people. From sages to servants, he listened actively, never ruling in arrogance.

Modern Insight: Good leaders listen to their team before making decisions. They respond, not dictate.

Try This:

- In your next meeting, speak last. Let others express their perspectives first.
- Ask: "What am I missing?" instead of "What do I think is right?"

2. Fairness Over Favoritism

Ram made tough decisions based on Dharma (righteousness), not personal preference. Even when it came to his own family — like the exile of Sita — he chose public duty over private emotion (though complex and debated, it reflected his commitment to perceived justice).

Modern Insight: In organizations or families, transparency and fairness build trust. Favoritism corrodes it.

Leadership Tip:

- Use frameworks, not emotions, to make decisions.
- Be open about how decisions are made, especially when they affect others deeply.

3. Everyone Has a Role

From Hanuman to Jambavan, every member of Ram's army had a defined, respected role. No one was too small or too mighty. Contributions were acknowledged equally.

Modern Insight: High-performing teams recognize that collaboration > hierarchy.

Team Culture Exercise:

- During weekly updates, have each team member highlight someone else's contribution.
- Celebrate silent contributors — not just the visible performers.

4. The Common Good Over Ego

Ram's rule was not about personal legacy but about public welfare. He made sacrifices to maintain harmony — even when misunderstood.

Modern Insight: Great leaders make uncomfortable but ethical choices when the team or organization is at stake.

Ask Yourself:

- "Is my decision for the greater good — or just my comfort zone?"

5. Justice With Compassion

Ram was just, but not cold. He forgave Ravana's brother Vibhishan and welcomed him. He gave people a chance to change, while holding them accountable.

Modern Insight: Combine accountability with empathy — especially with underperforming or struggling team members.

Tip for Managers:

- When giving feedback, sandwich it between care and clarity: "I see your effort. Here's what's missing. I believe in your ability to grow."

6. Inclusiveness and Empowerment

Ram gave leadership space to others — from Sugriv to Hanuman. He wasn't threatened by their strength; he enabled it.

Modern Insight: A true leader is not a bottleneck. They create other leaders.

For Team Leads or Parents:

- Let others take charge of projects or family decisions — and support them fully.

7. Building a Culture of Peace and Purpose

Ram Rajya wasn't perfect because of Ram alone. It worked because his values inspired the collective — ministers, citizens, even nature responded to the harmony.

Modern Insight: Culture is not created by slogans or rules, but by daily behaviour and emotional tone.

Reflection Point:

- What is the emotional climate you're creating around you?
- Are you instilling calmness, openness and growth — or fear, urgency and pressure?

The "Ram Rajya" Leadership Model

Pillar	**Modern Equivalent**
Dharma (Ethics)	Lead with fairness, not favoritism
Shravan (Listening)	Create safe spaces for others to speak
Tyag (Sacrifice)	Put collective needs above personal comfort
Sahyog (Cooperation)	Recognize and uplift every role in the team
Shanti (Peace)	Reduce chaos; lead with empathy and clarity

Final Reflection: You Don't Need a Throne to Build Ram Rajya

Ram Rajya isn't about kingship. It's a state of values — in your office, your home, or your heart. It starts not with laws, but with leadership that inspires trust.

"You build Ram Rajya not when others follow you out of fear, but when they stand beside you in faith."

Chapter 20

THE LEGACY OF RAM — LIVING WITH CHARACTER, EVEN WHEN NO ONE IS WATCHING

"Reputation is what people think of you. Character is what you are when no one is watching."

Introduction: What Remains When Power Fades?

Lord Ram's legacy is not confined to temples, hymns, or sculptures — it lives on through the values he embodied in silence, away from crowds, accolades, or battlefield victories. His decisions in moments of solitude — his commitment to truth, duty and sacrifice — reveal the deep moral compass that defined his character.

In a world of performance, metrics and public image, we ask:

What guides you when no one is watching?

1. Dharma Is a Personal Commitment, Not a Public Display

Ram did not perform for praise. He left the throne, accepted exile, kept promises and made painful sacrifices not for applause but because his inner values guided him.

Modern Insight: Your integrity is tested not during performance reviews or investor pitches, but when you quietly choose truth over ease — even if it costs you.

Try This:

Before a tough decision, ask: "What would I do if no one ever found out?"

2. Discipline Starts With the Self

Ram's greatest strength was self-control. He trained his body as a warrior, restrained his emotions as a king and reined in personal desires as a husband, son and leader.

Modern Insight: Daily discipline — waking early, sticking to principles, managing time — creates your legacy, not viral posts or big wins.

Action Habit:

- Build a non-negotiable morning habit that reflects inner discipline (e.g., 20 mins reflection, journaling, silence, or reading).

3. Choose the Right Over the Convenient

Ram chose exile over entitlement. He chose humility over resistance. These were not easy — but they preserved his character.

Modern Insight: The shortcut may win you likes, but the long road builds identity. Entrepreneurs, students, or professionals with "Ram Mindset" choose ethics over short-term gain.

Quick Check-In:

- Next time you are faced with two options, ask: "Which path will let me sleep peacefully tonight?"

4. True Power Lies in Restraint

Ram never misused his strength. Even when he could have destroyed his enemies instantly, he chose diplomacy, gave chances and practiced restraint.

Modern Insight: In leadership, power isn't proven by how fast you respond — but by how wisely.

Practice Tip:

Delay reaction in emotionally charged situations. Respond after understanding, not impulse.

5. Legacy Isn't Left — It's Lived

Ram didn't plan a legacy project. He lived one, daily, through actions aligned with his inner compass. His legacy was not created for remembrance — but it became eternal because it was purely lived.

Modern Insight: You don't have to "build a personal brand" to be remembered. Live with character and your impact will echo.

Ask Yourself:

- "Am I making choices today that I'll be proud of ten years from now — even if no one sees them?"

The "Unseen Character" Framework

Trait	Daily Practice Suggestion
Integrity	Follow through on your word — even in small things
Self-awareness	Reflect daily: "Did I act in alignment with my values?"
Humility	Acknowledge mistakes quickly and without defense

Trait	Daily Practice Suggestion
Courage	Stand up for truth, even when uncomfortable
Restraint	Avoid reacting when angry or insulted — pause first

Final Reflection: The Real Ram Lives Within You

Lord Ram's story is not just of a divine being — it is a mirror for our own lives. In every situation where you're tempted to compromise your principles, Ram's mindset reminds you that:

"It is not what you do in front of others that defines you, but what you choose when only your conscience is watching."

Your leadership, relationships, business and personal journey may not be sung in epic poems — but when built on inner character, it becomes divine in its own right.

Closing Thoughts

This is not the end of Lord Ram's journey — it's the beginning of yours.

The Ram Mindset is a call to live your life not in pursuit of perfection, but with purpose, discipline and quiet courage — no matter your path.

Chapter 21

BECOMING RAM — INTEGRATING VALUES, LEADERSHIP & PURPOSE IN MODERN LIFE

Introduction — The Journey from Inspiration to Identity

Every person admires Ram — but very few become like Him.
It's not His power we seek… it's His principle-driven life.

Ram teaches us:

- Dharma is not a speech — it is a choice you make every day.
- Leadership is not a position — it is responsibility.
- Strength is not loud — it is silent discipline.

This chapter is your final step — from knowing Ram's qualities to living them.

The Ram Identity Formula

To truly adopt The Ram Mindset, anchor your life in the 3 Pillars:

Pillar	What It Means	Modern Application
Dharma	Values, integrity & ethical decision-making	Choose the right path even under pressure
Leadership	Service, accountability, influence	Lead by example at home & at work
Purpose	Direction, meaning & long-term mission	Work toward a life that outlives you

When these three align —

you don't just follow Ram…you become like Ram. Becoming Ram in Daily Life

Ask yourself three questions every morning:

1. What is the right thing to do today? → Dharma
2. Who can I support or uplift today? → Leadership
3. How does today take me one step closer to my mission? → Purpose

A person who lives with these questions becomes:

- Emotionally balanced
- Professionally respected
- Personally peaceful

That is the Ram way of living.

What Changes When You Become Ram

Old Self	Ram Mindset Transformation
Reaction-driven	Response-driven
Self-centered	Value-centered
Fearful of results	Focused on right action
Seeks validation	Seeks excellence
Blames others	Accepts responsibility

Ram shows us:

- Success is temporary
- Character is permanent

Leadership Truth: People Follow Your Character

Modern workplaces reward skills…but promote character.

You don't need a title to lead. Every time you:

- Keep your word.
- Support your team.
- Take responsibility before reward

You move closer to Ram Rajya leadership.

"Do what is right, especially when no one is watching —That's where true greatness is born."

The Emotional Discipline of Ram

Even in exile…

Even in loss…

Even in war…

Ram never allowed his emotions to override Dharma.

In today's world:

- Deadlines = stress
- Rejection = anxiety
- Competition = insecurity

But Ram teaches:

"Strength is not controlling others. Strength is controlling yourself."

Purpose: The Fuel of a Legendary Life. Without purpose, we only survive.

With purpose, we serve. Your purpose may not be a kingdom…It may be your family, career, community, or service.

What matters is:

- Is your purpose bigger than your ego?
- Does it uplift others along the way?

Ram lived for something beyond Himself. That is why we remember Him today.

ACTION PLAN: Become Ram in 21 Days

A simple but powerful transformation challenge:

Day Range	Focus
Days 1–7	Practice **Dharma** in small decisions
Days 8–14	Lead with humility & accountability
Days 15–21	Align actions to your long-term purpose

If you give 21 days, Ram will give you a lifetime of clarity.

Reflection Prompts

Journal nightly (3 minutes):

1. Did I live by my values today? Where did I compromise?
2. How did I serve or uplift someone today?
3. What step did I take toward my mission?

These questions build character and self-awareness — the foundation of Ram Rajya within.

You Promise, Close your eyes and place your hand on your heart. Repeat silently:

"I choose the right path over the easy path. I lead with service. I live with purpose. I walk the path of Ram."

This promise is not a ritual. It is a rebirth of identity.

Final Thoughts

The Legacy Begins with You
"Ram did not become great because He won battles. He became great because He never lost Himself."

If you:

- Stand for Dharma
- Lead with compassion
- Act with purpose

Then you are already…Becoming Ram. And one day, someone will say:
"Because of you, I believe in goodness."
That will be your legacy.

ABOUT THE AUTHOR

Nikhil Kumar is a seasoned Product Manager in the IT industry, known for combining modern strategy with timeless wisdom. A modern thinker, spiritual learner and leadership enthusiast, Nikhil brings a unique perspective to solving today's real- world challenges by drawing from ancient Indian epics like the Ramayana.

With hands-on experience in Product Management, cross-functional leadership and business transformation, he has spent years guiding teams and professionals through complexity with clarity and purpose. His passion lies in helping individuals cultivate inner discipline, emotional intelligence and moral leadership—values he believes are more relevant today than ever before.

Through The Ram Mindset, he bridges the gap between mythological insights and practical life, offering actionable takeaways for entrepreneurs, changemakers and working professionals.

When he's not leading product initiatives or mentoring others, Nikhil loves reading spiritual texts, practicing self-reflection and creating frameworks that empower people to live and lead with intention.